Pure Majek

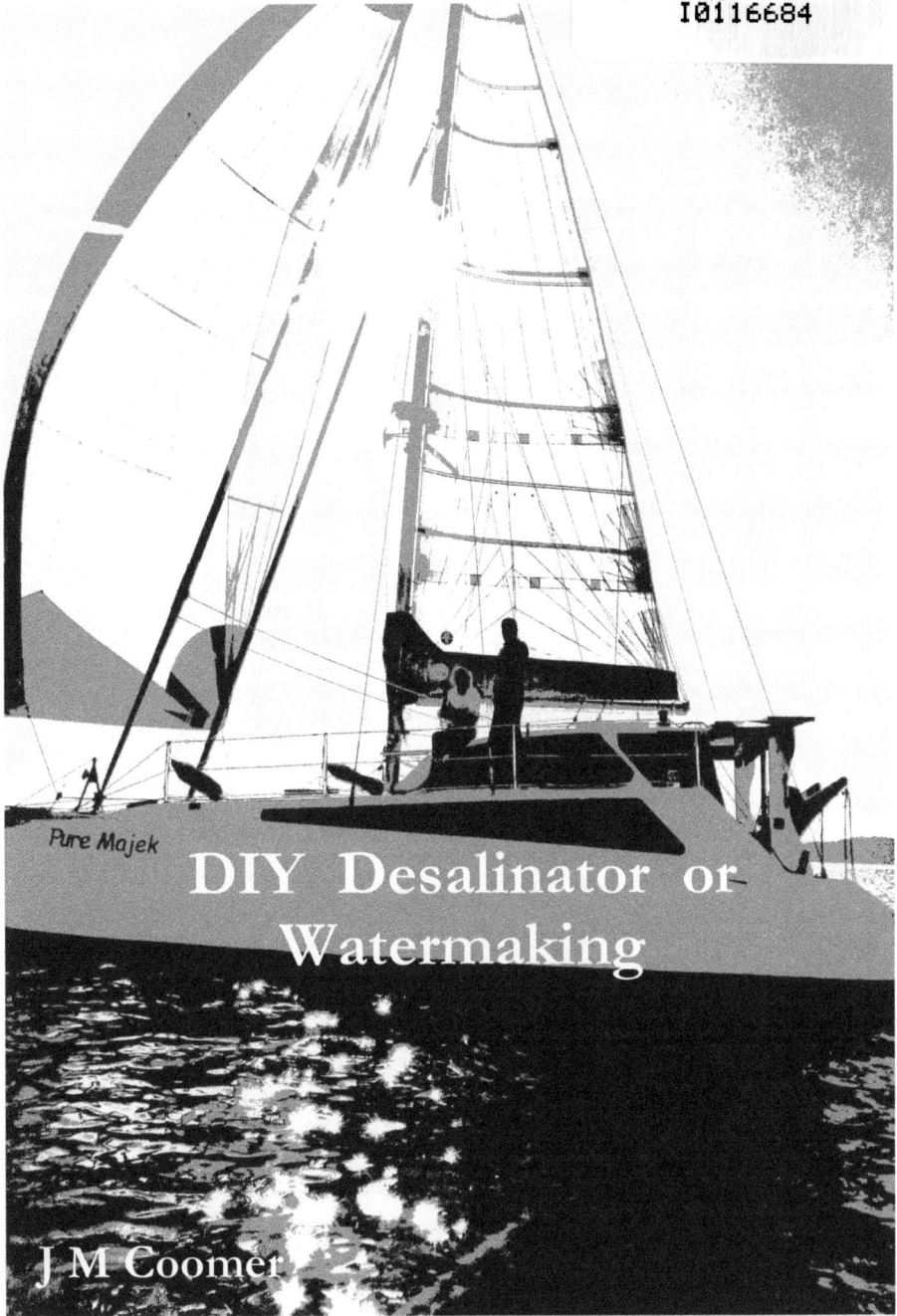

DIY Desalinator or Watermaking

J M Coomer

Copyright and Reproduction Rights

Copyright © 2012 James Coomer
E-mail: mail@diycatamaran.com
Website: www.diycatamaran.com

A cataloguing-in-Publication record is available
at the National Library of Australia
www.librariesaustralia.nla.gov.au

ISBN: 978-0-9874060-1-9

Preface

This writing is intended to provide a practical and informative tool for amateur DIY boatbuilders.

Here we have jotted how and why we tackled certain challenges with pointers that may assist others.

These notes are not intended to replace any popular building methods, rather supplement the decision making process of those currently in use.

Understanding how the water making process works, allows an informative decision for those who are moving this way.

We heavily researched the topic, then worked backwards tracking down components and analysing their importance in the 'big picture'. Depending on the output volume one needs, will dictate the size. An Internet search will soon show the very steep cost gradient and there is a reason for this, which we discuss too.

There is a lot of effort required to build a unit, but 100 litres of fresh water an hour is very achievable and worth the effort in financial outlay.

We also take a peek at refurbishing a commercial unit that utilises 'ERS', an energy saving function, reducing pipe pressures and power requirements.

James Coomer
www.diycatamaran.com

Table Of Contents

Chapter One:
What is Desalination?

Our attempts to find a reasonably priced desalinator unit that delivered large amounts of water over a short 'engine-running' period, did not prove fruitful.

In early 2000, the United States appeared to lead the way with their availability of desalinator components.

This, for the non-US resident, presented another challenge in that postage of these heavy 'complete units' would fast out way the search.

Making our own fresh water seems to supplement the solar energy charging of our batteries. The feeling of self-sufficiency and not being dependent on someone else to survive is a good one.

The Internet age and ability to freight small items worldwide has opened doors for the amateur builder and with a little drive and know-how,

a homemade desalinator is within reach. This is our successful attempt of how we went about the challenge.

We have since tackled another project (July 2011) and have successfully restored a 12vDC watermaker that provides 16 litres of water per 6 Amp hours.

It's from the Italian Schenker Watermaker Group and what a win that was. We discuss this in a later section. Please check the website (www.diycatamaran.com) for updates on this desalinator.

----- : -----

We planned to have plenty of freshwater. It meant *re-inventing the wheel* with desalination and trying to recover some of the high expense in this area by building the desalination unit ourselves.

Our original question was '*why was*

it so expensive?' The answer lies, we suspect, in the possible litigation issues of malfunctioning units and component compounds used in their construction, both of which we could tackle.

We scoured the Internet for desalinator units, which all ranged between AUD$5000 to AUD$15000 (July 2007), but with many of these packages, there was no generator or battery source as part of that package, only adding to our financial woes.

...become increasingly harder to claim component failure without receipted components...

Building a unit ourselves was the only viable alternative.

----- : -----

So what is it about these components that add to the cost? A 'safety model' put forward by Professor James Reason may help explain this quandary.

His theory of system failure, sometimes called the 'Swiss Cheese Theory', states that overall system failure is more often than not a function of many smaller failures.

These smaller failures may be as minute as a fatigued section caused by simple flexing which on its own, will not normally cause a failure.

But, when many small failures align (like the odd occasion when all the holes aligning in a block of Swiss cheese - the cheese collapses in that aligned area) and this too is the case in some manufactured desalinator units.

This is well documented in the aviation industry where accidents can often be traced back to a small component issue, which finally leads to the accident.

Applying this theory to the desalinator build meant that each component needed to be specifically chosen for its qualities.

Modification of these components, such as switching to a cheaper part or replacing a stainless steel nut with a plastic nut, will add to the holes in our block of 'desalinator Swiss cheese'.

A good example here concerns fittings below the waterline. While plastics development has come forward in leaps and bounds, even reputable pump manufacturers such as Jabsco with their 'cyclone range', state that plastic fittings should not be used below waterline on their pumps.

...designs are built with a certain safety reserve...

It's the continual small vibration of the motor, causing small fatigue lines in the fittings that when aligned with other fatigued components could cause a situation where the boat leaks and heaven forbid, sinks.

----- : -----

By nature, we (human beings) will always try and find an alternative or cheaper way to do or repair an item and this 'calculated risk' needs to be just that...very carefully calculated.

Replacing an elbow with a cheaper alternative may work at the start, but as contaminants fill the filters, the pump works harder and this in turn raises unnecessary pressure within those components.

Variations in water temperature causing expansion and contraction of the component add another hole to the fracture theory and eventually all the hard work comes undone, costs go up and the manufacturer becomes the easiest scapegoat for one's shortcutting.

A good excuse, except insurance assessors are now wise to this and it has become increasingly harder to claim component failure without receipted components.

For the reason mentioned above, many designs are built with a certain safety reserve, such as the motors horsepower - always higher than that actually required or piping that carries 30% higher-pressure ratings than what are actually listed.

...the manufacturer becomes the easiest scapegoat for one's shortcutting...

They do this for a reason.

Those who test these boundaries appear be the minority and are the ones we consistently meet conducting repairs and complaining of how labour intensive the desalination task is.

When you dig a bit further you find the dollars they saved initially during set-up, come home to roost.

Understanding some of this waffle will go a long way in helping grasp why certain items appear to be over-the-top with our choices and as stated previously, there are many ways to skin-a-cat when making a desalinator, and this is our way.

----- : -----

So, what is Desalination?

Desalination is the removal of impurities (such as salt) from a liquid. This then makes the water potable and/or palatable. Also called a Water Maker (or watermaker) , the desalinator is still fairly expensive due to the limited scope of development.

To date the cheapest way to do this has been by forcing the 'liquid form' through membranes that are small enough to remove the impurities.

This is a lot easier said than done as the pressure that is normally used to do this is around 56bar (around 820psi), fairly high and almost explosive when using inadequate components.

...'our boat – our wish-list'. ..

This then means that the vessel container must carry a higher pressure rating than its membrane, in our case, 68bar (around 1000psi).

We are talking very high compressed water pressures here, and this can be very dangerous in the wrong hands.

----- : -----

Calculating the freshwater needs

The summary of the desalination argument was that we needed to generate sufficient fresh water to cover our use, not that we have anything against those who enjoy the spiritual virtues of salt-water bathing.

For the seasoned sailor, the next few paragraphs are not for you. However, for the amateur builder hoping to win the heart of his water-loving wife/partner and kids, continue reading.

We jotted down the water requirements we thought would be our comfortable minimum per person. In line with Nigel Calders' suggestion we added a further 10% buffer, then multiplied this by the number of members in the family.

Our calculations are based on 4 showers per day plus drinking water. We used 22 litres per person as a guide making our requirements 88 litres per day for four adults.

...only 12-15% of saltwater taken through the high-pressure membrane is returned as fresh water...

We can see some already raising an

eyebrow, all we say is ìour boat - our wish-listî.

The other requirement we put in place was the running of a generator to drive the desalinator. It was not to exceed one hour a day - period.

Again, *'our boat - our wish-list'*, and for the sake of peace and quiet too.

This figure then represents a minimum freshwater requirement per day and becomes a key for calculations further on.

To calculate freshwater tank size, we then multiplied the daily figure by two. That would give us a comfortable two days of freshwater or a good six days if rationed supplies with a non-functioning desalinator were that to ever eventuate.

We have also a second 150-litre tank for the extended trip.

----- : -----

Pointers:

1. Minimum of 820psi pressure is needed for most desalination.

2. Calculate your minimum water quantity per day.

Traps:

1. Not realising the consequences of a burst high-pressure line.

Chapter Two:
Understanding System Make-up

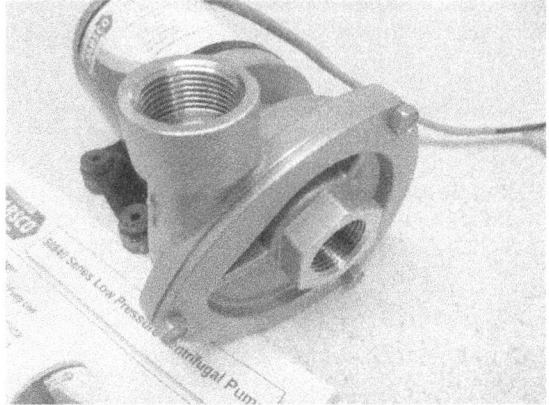

Use the 'Desalination Diagram' (next page), as a mud-map while you read this and the Components Chapters.

----- : -----

Simple System Operation

Saltwater is drawn into a Low Pressure Pump (called LPP here) via a Raw Water Filter.

The Raw water filter (one of three) removes larger debris and smaller crustaceans. This should have a removable filter that can be washed and or replaced easily.

The LPP delivers the water at around 9psi.

----- : -----

This low-pressure seawater is then again filtered before going to the High Pressure Pump (called HPP here).

The filters (two and three of three) are the larger canister household types that carry 5 and 10-micron filters respectively.

----- : -----

Depending on the power source, the HPP is engaged on and off via a Clutch (not shown in the Desalination Diagram). Some units can be purchased without a clutch. We chose the clutch type, the reasons are discussed later.

----- : -----

The high-pressure seawater from the HPP is then forced through Membranes, which separates the contaminants.

Only 10-15% of the HPP water entering the membranes will be returned as fresh water.

This can be measured via a

flowmeter (if installed).

----- : -----

The remaining HPP (80-85% of the intake water - now called brine), is returned to the sea via the High Pressure Regulator and its own Flow meter.

This return 'Brine' flow is very important as it in turn acts as flushing liquid within the membrane, self-cleaning the membrane of contaminants and venting them overboard.

----- : -----

A clear understanding of this basic sequence will help describe the components discussed next.

Another item mentioned shortly is the 'Motor'. Where this term is used, it specifically describes an electric or petrol motor that is used to drive the HPP.

-----: -----

Pointers:

1. Only 10 - 15% of inlet water will be freshwater.

2. The Membrane will need to be flushed <u>at least</u> every 7 days.

Traps:
1. Not ensuring filters are cleaned on a regular basis, especially if not used very often.

2. Not flushing the membrane.

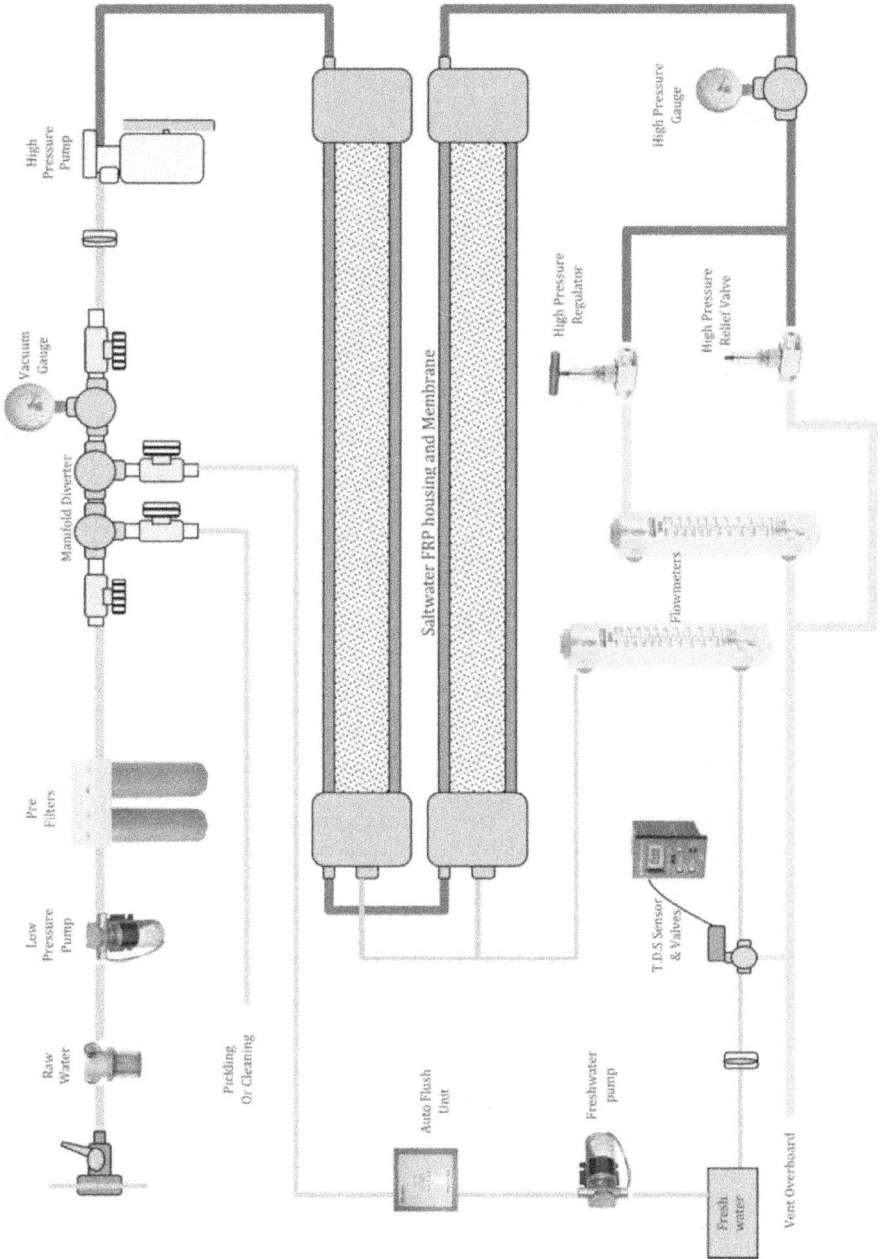

High Pressure Pump

Vacuum Gauge

Manifold Diverter

Pre Filters

Low Pressure Pump

Raw Water

Pickling Or Cleaning

Saltwater FRP housing and Membrane

High Pressure Gauge

High Pressure Regulator

High Pressure Relief Valve

Flowmeters

Auto Flush Unit

Freshwater pump

T.D.S Sensor & Valves

Fresh water

Vent Overboard

Desalination Diagram

13

Chapter Three:
Basic System Components

Use the 'Desalination Diagram' (previous page), as a mud-map while you read this section. It will help immensely.

----- : -----

High Pressure Pump (HPP)

The time that one wishes to have a motor purring (rumbling, vibrating or pumping fumes) needs to be carefully assessed as this will reflect the pump size that needs to be purchased.

Our choice limited this noise to one hour per day.

This meant that in 40 minutes, we had to generate all the water we needed to top up the tanks. The other 20 minutes of the 1-hour run time was to be used for any charging or

240VAC requirements, such as a washing machine.

For those about to start the *'numbers journey'* themselves, you will soon notice the challenges about to be faced in selection of a high pressure pump, pump motor and whether AC or DC motors should be used.

----- : -----

Given that we required 88lt/hr. freshwater, we needed a pump that could produce this, plus move an additional 85% more saltwater through the membranes.

Remembering that only 12-15% of

saltwater taken through the high-pressure membrane is returned as fresh water, making our high pressure pump requirements.

If:
    15 % = 88lt freshwater, then
    100% = 587lt total water needed
        (say 600lt/hr.).

This is a lot of water, yet alone in 40 minutes.

----- : -----

We are now starting to talk serious big pumping numbers.

To be able to do this, we used a type of pump is known as a 'high pressure pump' (HPP) as it increases saltwater inlet pressure from low pressure (around 0.55 bar (8psi)) to high pressure (no more than 65 bar (950psi)).

...Brass and saltwater
do not mix...

This is required to force saltwater through the membranes. While 65 bar (950psi) is a little high, we insert a High Pressure Regulator to lower this pressure to around 56 bar (820psi).

This 56 bar (820psi) figure is the magical minimum number required to bring the salinity of the saltwater down to an acceptable drinking water value.

This *drinking-water-value* is around 200 parts per million or less (saltwater being up around the 12,000 parts per million normally).

From these numbers above, it can be seen that a lot of contaminants need to be removed.

----- : -----

The pump used in desalination units is a specialised piece of equipment and needs to be stainless steel or bronze.

Any other material compounds will not be suitable for saltwater use, and yes, this definitely includes brass (found in most high pressure water washers).

Brass and saltwater do not mix.

There are some good and bad high-pressure pump manufacturers out there, too. We narrowed our search down to AR Pumps, Cat Pumps, and General Pumps.

Our final choice was a Cat Pump given that many of the off-the-shelf desalinator companies use Cat equipment.

The decision now was whether to go Stainless Steel or Bronze HPP pump parts.

The Cat Pump Company state that:

'Some installations and water
conditions may tolerate a liquid-end
construction of nickel aluminium bronze.
Other locations may demand more
corrosion-resistant liquid-end materials
such as 316SS, Duplex Stainless Steel or
even Super Duplex for the RO pump.

A lower speed (rpm) for your RO pumps
is highly recommended. When pumping
corrosive liquids such as seawater,
higher rpm operation further aggravates
the corrosion-erosion wear process
initiated by seawater'.

The cost of the various HPP types does vary from vendor to vendor and bronze is cheaper by 20%, so it pays to shop around.

A close search was made for a second hand HPP unit on Ebay and we did find a few. BUT, with all of them:

➢ Do the internal components need replacing?

➢ Has the pump been dropped?

➢ Has the pump seized?

(One respondent here stated 'no, I canstill turn it with a wrench') etc.

We could not get a component guarantee for this critical high-pressure part, which is why we chose to buy new (remembering the Swiss Cheese theory discussed earlier).

----- : -----

HPP cavitation is one item that should be considered during this building phase, cavitation being influenced by air seeping into the system plumbing.

...cavitation is one item that should be considered during this building...

Plumbing must contain suitable shutoff valves to prevent air from entering the HPP unit at all costs. This also means that plumbing must be very secure and the use of PTFE liquid or tape is strongly recommended.

Air here definitely does fast-track premature wear and resultant costs as well as frustration with repairs.

We settled on purchasing the Cat Pump 3-Frame Plunger Pump-Model 241 (in Stainless Steel). The specification sheet for the 241 HPP

recommended that:

> The unit be driven by a minimum of 3.0hp electric motor

> An operating pressure range is 70bar (1000psi) to 85bar (1200psi) (We chose to use the 70bar figures) and for this pressure,

> The HPP operating RPM of 1725 was needed. This figure will be used later in sizing the motor pulley.

Note too that the manufacturer has made the clear distinction between electric and gas engines, electric being their preferred choice for advertising reasons. This leads us onto the next challenge where we discuss the this issue.

----- : -----

Motor to drive the HPP

The motor that drives this HPP unit can be:

> Electric DC (directly connected to the HPP pump),

> Electric AC (directly connected to the HPP pump),

> Belt-drive from an electric motor, or from a

> Belt-drive petrol (diesel) generator.

The choices are varied and can be very confusing to the uninitiated.

One option available to us was to use:
> A petrol (gas) engine, to drive
> An electric motor, to run
> The HPP

We found that the amount of petrol (gas) engine power required to run a largish electric motor (3hp in our case with the 241 Cat pump), was enormous.

In fact, electric motors become veryrestrictive beyond 1-1.5hp electric motor sizes, which is why many tend toward the belt-drive units.

Another option was the AC Electric Motor on its own. Given that we only have batteries, an Inverter would be needed.

The challenge with AC motors is that they need three times their running power requirement just to break the inertia during their initial start-up.

Don't be fooled by this requirement. There is much written about it. If in doubt, ask any electrician who is familiar with AC electric motors of this size.

----- : -----

As a rough guide, this meant that to start 3hp electric motor, one would need an equivalent 5-6hp AC electric motor 'power-draw' just to get it started (while not strictly correct, this acts as a very good guide).

Then you need to factor in the 1-hour running battery 'power-draw' to make the required water.

We were often asked why we could not use a 2kva Honda power generator to do the job.

We came to the conclusion that it would only be able to drive a small HPP, say 10 - 20lt per hour, making running times a lot longer (for our requirements) and in some cases more expensive.

----- : -----

Other avenues we did look at were 'soft-starters' which proved well in theory, but as we found out would not be suitable for an amateur desalinator build.

We finally agreed that we needed a non-electric motor with a belt-drive system. Searching for this took some time.

Our decision to minimise holes in the hull meant that saltwater cooling became a last resort and left freshwater or fan cooled motors our preferred option.

Given that our HPP needed a 2.5HP Electric Motor, an increase of 20% is needed for the petrol (gas) equivalent, making our Petrol Motor minimum size of 3HP.

This was stipulated in the manufacturers data sheet downloaded from the Internet.

To this, one needs to consider how hard they want the motor to work and do they want to use the same motor for other applications.

Finally, our choice was between the industrial diesel fresh water-cooled generators from a Yanmar (TF60 - 67kg) or the unleaded air-cooled industrial Honda (GX200QXE - 26kg).

Weight and cooling requirements dictated the direction here as they were the same price.

Motor - Honda GX200QXE

Motor - Yanmar TF60

The Honda GX200QXE is a common unit and parts are very readily available and are cheap to buy. It also has electric start, which could come in handy depending on the automation level that one desires.

We went with the Honda.

It has a maximum shaft RPM (with no load) of 3900RPM. As we do not want maximum RPM and given that petrol (gas) engines struggle with torque below 50% of their normal operating range, we chose 60% of this value - 2400RPM.

According to Honda dealership, this happens to be:
> The most fuel economic range for the motor,
> Reduces wear and tear of the motor components,
> Allows the motor to run cooler, and
> Reduces the noise level by 15%.

This 2400-RPM will be used later to calculate the motor pulley size.

----- : -----

12vDC Clutch/Pulley

Options were available for a:
> Direct-drive 'pulley belt' system, or
> Clutch-drive 'pulley belt' system.

We chose the Cat Pumps Industrial Clutch - Model 34961, which has a 7î OD (outer diameter).

This is an important OD number needed for calculating the Motor Pulley size in the next section.

Cat Pumps Industrial Clutch - Model 34961

The clutch is a real asset and allows the motor to be run without the HPP engaged making the motor available as a generous generator (alternator actually) and could also be used to:
> Power 240V in times of need (thinking of a washing machine here - remembering now that fresh water will not be a issue),
> The far reaching 'wish-list' item for air-compressor ability for scuba units,
> Provide power for a small air conditioner/ heater, and/or
> As back up for those overcast days for the batteries.

----- : -----

Clutch engagement occurs when a small amount of 12vDC power is applied via a separate switch from the battery.

While ever this switched battery power is available the clutch will remain engaged running the HPP.

Cut the switched power and the clutch will disengage stopping the HPP. The motor will continue to run until switched off separately.

This leads into our next consideration, HPP pump protection via automatic shutdown.

----- : -----

This is not mandatory - but a nice-to-have. Inserting a pressure switch in the salt water feed line from the LPP to the filters, will detect:
> A failed LPP (pump could fail or, pump could not be switched on),

and
> Low water pressure (the inlet or raw water strainer could have blocked with debris).

This 'pressure switch' would cut electrical power to the 12vDC clutch achieving the automatic disconnection; thereby stopping the HPP unit from running.

The motor will continue to run and the worst it can do is run out of petrol, which is fine. It's all about saving the HPP unit from water starvation.

...clutch is a real asset and allows the motor to be run without the HPP engaged...

This HPP decision was one of the stumbling blocks that took a few months to remedy and now having resolved the water requirements and HPP guidelines, the planning for the remainder of the items took off.

----- : -----

Pulley; Motor Calculations

To calculate the motor pulley size, three figures are required from the previous data:
> Desired Motor RPM - 2400,
> Clutch/Pulley OD - 7î, an
> HPP 70bar (1000psi) RPM - 1725.

Motor Pulley OD

Jabsco 12vDC Puppy

$$= \frac{(\text{HPP Pulley OD} \times \text{HPP RPM})}{\text{Motor RPM}}$$
$$= \frac{(7 \times 1725)}{2400}$$
$$= 5.0\hat{i}$$

To summarise:
Operating the motor at 2400RPM, will turn the 5.0î and 7î belt pulley system.

This in turn will drive the HPP at 1725RPM producing 68bar (1000psi) of saltwater pressure to the membranes.

Accidental overpressure is covered in the 'Pressure Regulator' section later.

----- : -----

Low Pressure Pump (LPP)

This would be the second most critical component in the whole desalinator system.

Cheap alternative LPP's, will increase costs in future years in replacement parts.

The unit must be capable of providing a positive flow of corrosive fluid at a rate higher than that required by the manufacturer of the HPP.

During the planning stages, the flow rate should be calculated at a value, plus 15%. This 15% then covers:
> Filtration losses as the filter progressively fouls,
> Saltwater temperature variations,
> Desalinator height above the waterline, and
>Aging of components, both within the LPP and upstream of the strainer.
Note that we talk of a high flow rate here, not a high-pressure rate.

A pressure rate around 0.55 bar (8 psi) would be sufficient as long as up-line the filters are regularly cleaned and there are at least two in series.

Failure of the LPP at any stage could cost in repair as the feed source of the whole system now stops.

The HPP will end up trying to operate with a negative pressure, have possible air ingestion, and damage the pumping components, specifically the membranes.

This means that while the HPP is operating, someone must continually be in attendance at all times or, a safety feature installed (such as a pressure switch) that can initiate automatic shutdown of the HPP unit should the LPP fail.

----- : -----

This too is not mandatory, however we chose to install a pressure switch/sensor.

At low LPP pressure, a sensor cuts the 12vDC circuit to the clutch,

disengaging the clutch to the HPP. Simple yet effective.

LPP line pressure greater than 0.1 bar (1.5 psi) closes the 12vDC clutch electrical circuit via the pressure switch.

Once the clutch power switch is switched to on, power flows through the pressure switch to the clutch and engages the clutch. This in turn allows the HPP to operate until either:
> The clutch power is switched off , or,
> The pressure switch is < 1.5psi.

The petrol/diesel motor will continue to run with no damage to any components until:
> It runs out of fuel (gas), or
> It is switched off.

For those really keen, another pressure switch could be installed in the freshwater tank, so that a filled tank would disengage the clutch once again.

----- : -----

Two LPP pump types are available here:
>A centrifugal type pump, or
>A self-priming non-centrifugal unit.

The self-priming units (positioned above the waterline) normally require twice as much preventative maintenance due the wear on the impeller.

Centrifugal pumps however, must be installed below waterline and for this reason, do not require priming and there is a lot less impeller maintenance required.

We chose Jabsco 12vDC Puppy Pump for this purpose and while expensive, forms a key component in the set-up that can have minimal maintenance.

Centrifugal pumps can be run normally with little to no flow. This can be a huge advantage as the LPP can be used to purge the pipes to the HPP without the HPP running.

This prevents air from entering the HPP system, saving on the life of the membranes.

...continual opening and closing, will take its toll on the seacock unless correctly installed ...

----- : -----

Seacock

So do we use stainless steel, bronze or plastic?

As far as we were concerned, in our situation, stainless steel or bronze would be fine.

Our frequent use at this inlet required the seacock to be firmly installed. This meant no physical movement each time the seacock was opened or closed.

...a vacuum gauge for visual filter indication, prompting filter maintenance...

The seacock is closed after each use, purely for reason of safety, due to the time we spend away from the vessel.

Additionally, our yacht could beach at low tide exposing the inlet point and a slow drain of piped water will occur.

If the seacock were not closed each time, this would require bleeding of air each time we used the unit,

Perko Marine Deacock

making the process very cumbersome and even more complicated.

A simple safe solution - we see it as easy 'Insurance'.

This continual opening and closing, will take its toll on the seacock unless correctly installed on a very solid base.

----- : -----

Filtration(1 of 3)
Raw Water Strainer

We found that options here are limited and expensive.

Given that the pressure in the lines prior to the Low Pressure Pump (LPP) are very low around 0.55 bar (8 psi), a standard plastic strainer from a reputable manufacturer (such as Shurflo) could be an alternative to the bronze types sold by Perko or Groco.

This flies against that recommended by some LPP manufacturers, so be cautious and do the homework. It needs to be capable of passing 100lts of water at a minimum.

The Filter insert should be of the stainless steel type and easily replaceable.

Diverging a little, while meandering through a scrap metal yard one afternoon, we stumbled across a container of discarded 60-micron fine mesh.

The off-cuts were remnants of material used to prevent termite and ant infestation, commonly called Termi-mesh.

It just happens that this is also stainless steel too, so we now have a lifetime replacement supply of filter mesh.

Strainer units with a bowl at the base make it very easy for cleaning and the odd mudskipper or snail can be quickly removed before decomposition occurs.

This component should be installed in a position below waterline that is easily accessible and can get the odd splash of saltwater during filter cleans.

An upstream shut-off valve can be very helpful here too, to minimise fluid loss during filter cleaning or LPP repair.

----- : -----

Filtration (2 & 3)
Fine Micron

This is provided by way of three 10-inch canisters, two canisters for desalination filtration, and one for mains water filling.

Firstly mains water, this contains chlorine, which is very harmful to the membranes and must therefore be removed prior to being placed in the tanks.

This unit contains a good quality carbon filter.

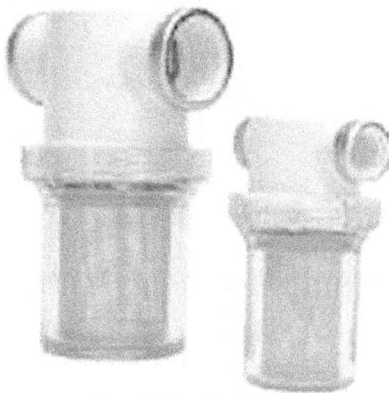

Raw Water Strainer

Pentek Canister Filters

24

One would think that this would normally not be a concern but remember that freshwater from the freshwater tanks is used to flush the components and purge the units for short-term storage.

This includes the membranes and its here the damage occurs. To counter this, we have inserted a filter housing with a good quality carbon filter.

Once filling is complete, the carbon filter is removed and then dried for at least a week before storage.

The other two canisters must be capable of corrosive fluid transfer and carry a safety valve.

These too must be in a very easily accessible position for maintenance, some saltwater will also be lost below the canisters during the filter changes.

The filter housings should be moulded from polypropylene and carry O-rings in the lid. These units will house 10 and 5-micron filters respectively.

To prolong the life of the membrane and system components, it is necessary to monitor the sediment collection of the filters.

One way is to maintain a log detailed further on in this section, or an alternative way is to install a vacuum gauge for visual filter indication, prompting filter maintenance.

The initial expense was worth every cent. As the filters soil, the Vacuum indication will increase.

With a little trial and error, a figure can be worked and logged as the prompt for filter changing.

We chose a stainless steel 70mm face 0 to -1Bar Vacuum Gauge that we located on Ebay.

Make sure that it is glycerin filled as the vibration of the HPP and motor can make it vibrate to the point of destruction.

It is far more advantageous to be proactive with maintenance, rather than re-active with breakdowns. This would be a 'Desalination Log' item.

----- : -----

Desalinator Log

Maintaining a system specification log is very critical if the unit is hands on. The log should include all the filter sizes as well component replacement numbers.

This is especially important at the start stage of the new desalinator as it provides the foundation for the life of the components and their maintenance.

A section should also be maintained to monitor water quality with the handheld TDS meter and the time it takes to reach this level (not required if the system has an automated TDS sensor and Solenoid/motorized valve).

This is another indication of adverse sediment build-up within the filters (or within the membranes) and is a key to the change intervals required.

----- : -----

Membrane Housing

Housings come in many various shapes and sizes, the most common lengths being 14, 21, and 40-inch.

Then there are their diameters, which vary from 2î to 4î.

Our studies have shown little differences between sizes and diameters against effective use.

Pointers we have include the space available for a particular size and surface area available in the membrane.

...the prefix 'SW' on the membrane item number...

At the time of writing we found that an initial higher expense in the more popular 2.5î x 40î housings, linked in series proved cheaper in the long run with replacement membranes and as a last resort, redundancy.

In the event one membrane failed with no replacement membrane - just removing the membrane and continuing with the desalination on the remaining membrane will still provide fresh water at a reduced rate.

We found that increasing the number of housings did not increase the amount of freshwater given our careful planning of the pump size.

The additional housing may allow longer use of the membranes, however twice the membrane replacement cost.

Housings for high-pressure membranes (that are used in desalinators) are normally found in Stainless Steel or fibreglass.

Rigid PVC is an option that with the correct pressure rating could be used. We chose 2 x (2.5î x 40î) Fibreglass housings, commonly listed as FRP.

Our Pressure Vessels were purchased from American R.O. in the US and

Membranes and Housings

are Fibreglass PVF-2540 (x 2)

----- : -----

Membrane choice

Here there is a choice between saltwater units, brack-water, and standard house-water membranes.

All are specific; especially the saltwater units and these can sometimes be picked by the prefix 'SW' on the membrane item number.

It is important to ensure that this is closely followed, as error here will cost dearly down the line with component failure.

Other digits on the membrane can indicate their unit size (as in our case, 2540 indicates a 2.5î diameter x 40î long), simple when you know how. Not all membranes are listed like this though.

Our Membranes were purchased from American R.O. in the US and are Filmtec SW30-2540 (x 2).

----- : -----

Pressure Regulator

The pressure that the system operates at is variable. With the slow blocking of filters by contaminants, temperature, variation of pumps RPM and to a lesser extent, aging of the components, the system needs to be manually controlled.

The regulator should be stainless steel and able to withstand very high-pressure loads, in excess of 100bar (1450psi).

We purchased a new Cat Pump

Pressure Regulator - model 7066 for this purpose.

It should also have an easy usable strong knob, sounds silly - but not

Cat Pump Pressure Regulator - 7066

Typical Pressure Gauge

when ones hands are wet and fine adjustment is needed.

----- : -----

Pressure Gauge

We have inserted a pressure gauge in the brine line after the membranes to monitor and provide accurate system pressure indications.

27

The pressure gauge is stainless steel 70mm (0 - 100bar (1500psi)), which was again purchased off Ebay.

----- : -----

TDS Meter

A TDS meter measures the salinity of the water. We chose to automate our system and have included a TDS meter with controller power to activate a Solenoid N.O. selector valve.

TDS Controller BL 983319-0

Once a programmed value is met (i.e. 200ppm) the unit supplies power to activate an in-line valve allowing freshwater to be diverted to the tanks.

The unit we chose is made by Hanna and is a panel mounted TDS Controller BL 983319-0. Don't forget to order the TDS Probe HI 7634-00 at the same time.

----- : -----

Pointers:

1. Use only 'BSP threaded' or only 'NPT threaded' fittings.

2. Calculate your minimum water quantity per day.

3. Use the largest inlet size (1 1/2").

Traps:

1. Mixing thread types.

2. Making a too complicated unit,

Chapter Four:
Watermaker Automation

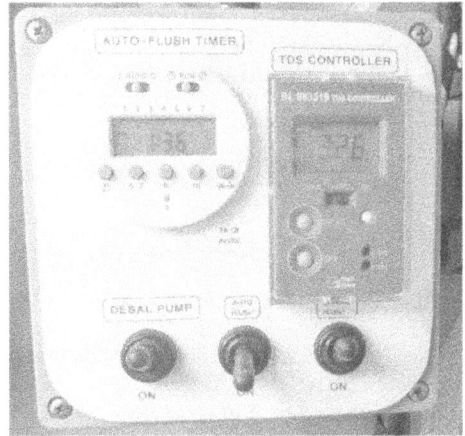

Auto Flush Computer

To be able to leave the yacht for periods exceeding four days between desalination making, we wanted the system automated.

A company called Quality Water Works makes a neat bit of gear that has a timer that can be set to flush the membranes.

All it needed was the ships normal freshwater pump system to operate. We purchased their Automatic Flush Module and have to say that they were very patient with our questioning.

Our Auto flush works by using the vessels own freshwater pump and existing tank water to flush the membranes at regular intervals. Once flushed, the water is vented overboard.

To accomplish this, the vessels

freshwater pump needs to be wired 'hot'.

By 'hot' we mean that it remains on continually when other electrical mains power is removed, such as switching off the main batteries switch when one leaves the vessel.

For those who have purchased 'A Sailing Catamaran Building Project', you will find an electrical circuit drawing called the 'Hot Battery Bus'.

The other important item is 'freshwater water in the tanks'.

Sufficient water needs to be present to flush the entire desalinator unit at regular intervals while away from the vessel.

Sounds silly and obvious, but with lack of water (or pumps running on an empty tank), will cause the fresh water pump to burnout.

It is very important that the flushing be done with NON-CHLORINATED water. Chlorine damages the membranes.

This links back to the Filter section discussed a few chapters back where we mentioned three canister filters. Two for the desalinator and the third filter carries a carbon insert to remove any tap water chlorine, if you choose to fill the tanks this way.

...third filter carries a carbon insert to remove any tap water chlorine...

The amount of water to do each flush needs to be calculated. We used a bucket to measure the wastewater during a trial run, and at the same time, timed the flush duration. The timer can then be set and we recommend a 4-day cycle or a particular flush duration.

----- : -----

Flow Meters

These units are used to provide a visual cue to the operation of the whole system. There are normally two placed in the system and the preferred position is 'panel-mounted' somewhere.

Panel mounting does incur additional plumbing requirements, but allows effective use of the flow meters.

The meters show freshwater output per minute and brine water output per minute, the latter having much higher flow increments per min or hour than its freshwater counterpart.

Qualities that we required within the gauge included:
> Stainless Steel float, float guides

and wetted parts (many have brass
or nickel coated brass),

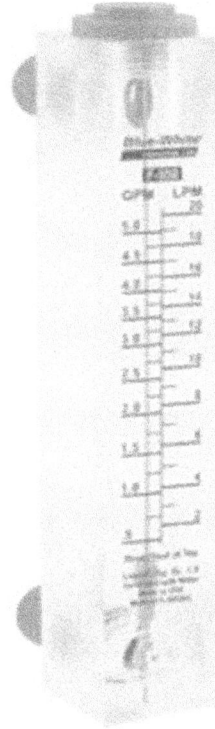

Blue White Rotameter - F550

> Acrylic frame,
> 125mm in length, and
> No valve
> Panel mounted

The most common gauging is in gallons per minute or gallons per hour (the US standard).

To remain within metric boundaries and based on the desalinator that we have built, we have chosen gauge ranges of:
> 1.5 - 18.0 Lpm (litres per minute), and
> 22 - 230 Lph (litres per hour)
> Alternative to Lph above:
> 0.4 - 4 Lpm (litres per minute)

There is also a Ccm range that can be used:
> 1500 - 19000 Ccm (cubic centimeters) and
> 23000 - 227000 Ccm (cubic centimeters)

The Flow Meters proved the hardest to track down. While there are a few quality manufacturers around many have agents throughout the world, some quick money-spinners and others better priced.

In all cases, it was cheaper to buy through the US with all shipping and insurance.

We chose the Blue-White F-550 (0.4 - 4 LPM) for the fresh waterside and the Blue-White F-550 (2 - 20 LPM) for the brine water.

The more common acrylic 'flow-meter' manufacturers include:
1. Dwyer - Visi float - VFB range .
2. Key Instruments - Flo-Rite series FR Flowmeters.
3. King Instruments - 7520-5C Series.
4. Omega Instruments - FL-2000 range.
5. Blue White Rotameter - F550 range.

----- : -----

Valves - Solenoid / Motorised

There are two main types of valves used with desalination units, those that are Motorised and those operated by a solenoid.

The main reason people choose one over the other is the speed of closing / opening of the valve.

The motorised units are a lot slower, anywhere from 4 - 12 seconds from one position to the other extreme. When compared to the solenoid speed of one second, there is a huge difference.

----- : -----

Motorised Solenoid Valve

Motorised Valves

These units are well-built and normally costly to purchase and replace when component failure is at hand.

Occasionally, it has been known for these valves to not function correctly or remain partially open.

Normally not too much of an issue however, when talking salinity in fresh water, these small malfunctions could wipeout 200lts of fresh water in 30 seconds.

Not only that, but if one has components in the fresh system that is not compatible, then there follows component failure (remembering back to the Desalinator Cheese theory).

----- : -----

Solenoid Valves

A solenoid valve is an electrical valve that uses a magnetic force via a small yet strong coil to open and close the valve.

...TDS unit will close the valve once the correct salinity is reached...

These types of valves are said to fail less and when they do, the parts are easily interchangeable.

While we would have preferred a stainless steel or bronze unit, they were outside our price range, so we settled for brass.

As the valve will be in the freshwater line only, we are not expecting any corrosion that is normally associated with saltwater and brass compounds.

The unit is a 'Normally Open' type (discussed below), which operates to a closed valve position when 12vDC power is applied.

Remove the power and the valve automatically opens allowing water to flow through. This is a fail-safe feature in the event of power loss.

The valve will open allowing water to be vented overboard instead of contaminating the fresh water tank.

Installation Theory:
Fresh water is routed vertically down 700mm directly below the membrane outlet and overboard.

A 'T' is placed on the inlet side of the valve and the valve placed in the line just before it vents overboard (roughly 600mm).

From that 'T' we turn the line back up 600mm then around and to the freshwater tank.

Theory at work:
Gravity will force the water *to take the most direct route* which is down the pipe, past the open 'T', through the solenoid valve and overboard.

The TDS unit (discussed later) will close the valve once the correct salinity is reached and water will be forced up the piping and finally through to the fresh water tank.

The solenoid type was our preferred when it comes to the automation of the TDS unit.

We managed to get four as a package off Ebay and will closely watch their wear with spares readily available.

----- : -----

Valve Terminology

Where one has an inlet and outlet and shuts the fluid off, this is known as a 2-way valve.

A 3-way valve has an additional outlet, sometimes called the diverter outlet. The other two ports being the inlet port and exhaust port.

The reason we make this statement is that an option exists whether these ports are open (called Normally Open or N.O.) or closed (called Normally Closed or N.C.)

Sometimes the fluid is used to operate (or assist in operating) the valve and this is called a Differential Operated valve.

Valves that operate on their own power are called Direct Acting Valves and are preferred in the build.

The shock here is the cost of these units. They range anywhere from AUD $300 - AUD $700 for the stainless steel units.

This put a totally different tack on the build and the way that our unit was designed; we only needed one for the TDS unit.

In summary, one should source:
> A stainless steel 2-way solenoid valve,

> N.O. - which makes it fail-safe to the open position if power is lost saving good water

> Largest in size - the larger the better,

> 12Vdc power operated, and

> Teflon (PTFE), where Stainless is not used

> Depending on position in the system, the correct pressure rating (+ 20% as a safety measure) must be considered.

----- : -----

Pressure Relief Valve

This component functions as a safety valve within the whole set-up monitoring:
> The 'Membrane Housing maximum pressure - rated to 68bar (1000psi),

> 'HPP Unit' maximum pressure - rated at 68bar (1000psi), and

> System pressure in the event of Pressure Regulator' failure.

It has been set to open at 66bar (960psi), venting brine water overboard, and closing at 55bar (800psi).

Here we have used the Swaglock SS-R4M8F8 with a purple spring. We

located these on Ebay.

----- : -----

Swaglock SS-R4M8F8

Mounting Frame

Our frame mounting has been cut from 10mm (5083 grade) Aluminum. While it sounds rather complicated, this was through choice.

We divided the desalinator into three units in an effort to minimize the space that the units occupy, they are:

> The Motor and HPP unit (double story to minimize space)

> Control Panel (has been separated to reduce vibration of the components), and

> Membrane unit.

If you are about to tackle this challenge, there are really no boundaries with the exception of the base, it needs to be extremely sturdy, and components must be bolted down securely.

----- : -----

Hoses - Joining the three Assemblies

The use of high pressure flexible hosing is strongly encouraged. Our ratings from the HPP to the membranes and then the Pressure Relief Valve are in excess of 135bar (2000psi).

The fittings proved to be the hardest part with these connections.

Flexible hosing is required given the movement around the various parts and a word of caution, if you intend fixing the tubing to a surface, ensure that it is within rubber grommets to stem the vibration.

----- : -----

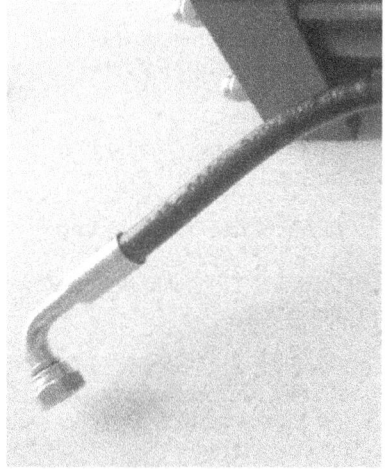

High Pressure piping and fittings

Chapter Five:
Electrical Ideas

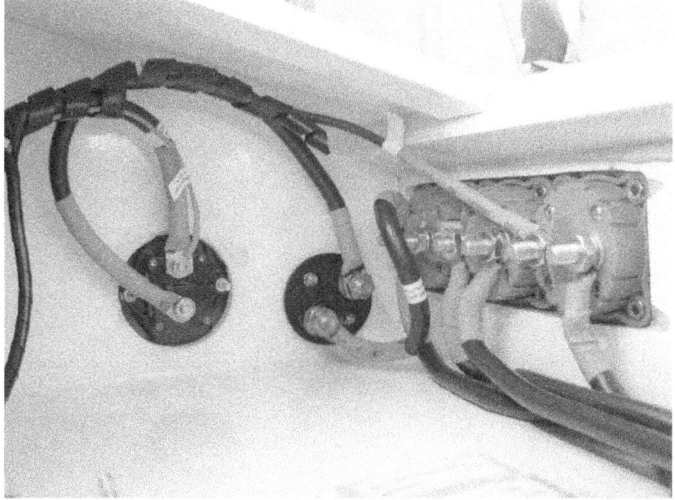

The electrical system works off a 'Hot Battery', which then covers power availability when on board (under normal operation) and while away (for auto-flushing of the membrane).

The 'Hot Battery' is a battery with connections that stay 'live' while away from the vessel.

In our case the Hot Battery Bus carries live power to the Bilge Pumps, Freshwater Pump, Auto Flush Controller & Navigation Panel (certain units that require continual power to maintain pre-set settings.

To disconnect the Hot Battery Bus (or HBB), we have installed an HBB Switch specifically for this purpose.

Our book 'A Sailing Catamaran Building Project' carries much more information on this topic.

With an HBB, the auto-flush controller can be programmed to flush periodically while away from the vessel with normal power off.

Auto flushing will require the vessels normal freshwater pump to run, which is why we have this connected to the HBB.

Please follow on the diagram on the next page.

----- : -----

The Hot Battery Bus is key to the whole electrical operation.

Freshwater Pump

The vessels normal water pump system is powered via a 10Amp circuit breaker.

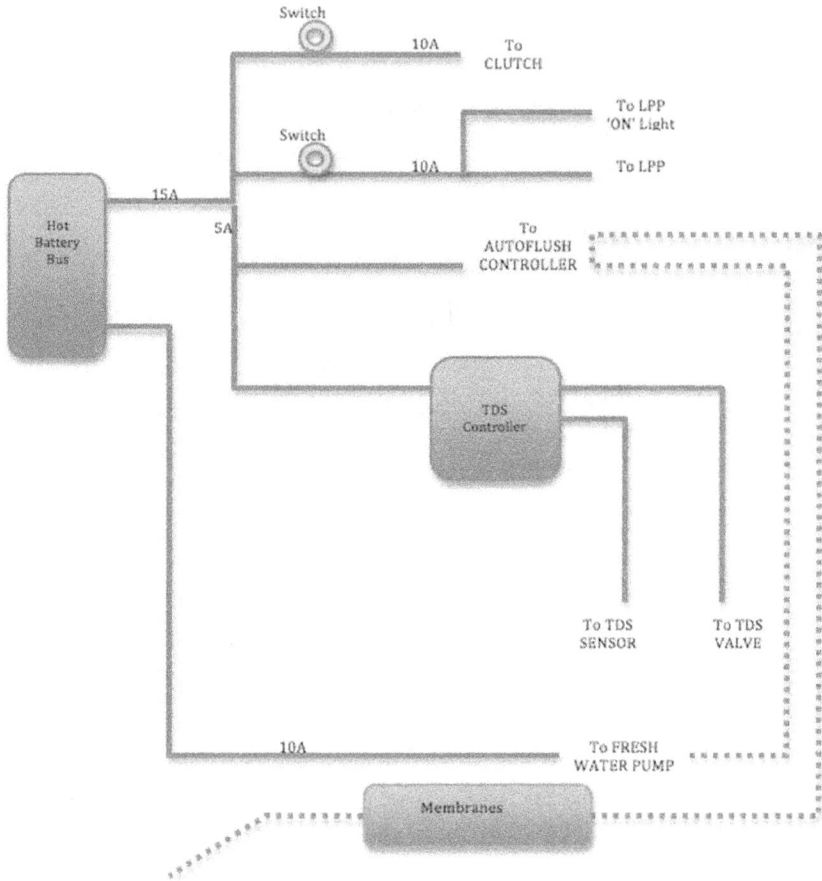

Switch

10A   To
CLUTCH

To LPP
'ON' Light

Switch

10A   To LPP

15A

5A   To
AUTOFLUSH
CONTROLLER

Hot
Battery
Bus

TDS
Controller

To TDS
SENSOR

To TDS
VALVE

10A   To FRESH
WATER PUMP

Membranes

Solid Line - Power to component
Dashed Line - Water flow on activation

Watermaker Electrical Diagram

This line remains pressurised at 6psi at all times. Any drop in line pressure will activate the pump to re-pressurise the line.

Under normal conditions, using any tap in the freshwater system inside the vessel will lower the water pressure, automatically activating the *freshwater pump* to ON to re-pressurise the line.

Alternatively, the same occurs when switching the *auto-flush controller*. Power opens the 12vDC auto-flush *water solenoid valve* (not shown) allowing water to flow to the membranes.

The *freshwater pump* senses the water pressure drop in the freshwater line re-pressurises the line.

De-activating the *auto-flush controller*, closes the *water solenoid valve* (not shown). The *freshwater pump* will continue to run until line pressure reaches 6psi, then the *freshwater pump* automatically switches OFF.

----- : -----

Powered via a 15Amp circuit breaker are the vessels:
> Desalinator Clutch,
> LPP Pump and LPP Light,
> Auto-Flush Controller, and
> TDS Controller.

Auto-Flush Controller
The *auto-flush controller* receives a open signal from the TDS controller. This allows power to OPEN the *water solenoid valve*.

When opened, the freshwater pump senses a pressure drop and it starts

to re-pressurise. The *freshwater pump* will then run until the valve is closed (or de-powered in this case).

This 6psi pressure is enough to flush the membranes on a regular basis.

The freshwater used is then vented overboard.

The TDS controller
The TDS controller can be programmed to supply power to 12vDC component. This has a seven-day automatic program.

We have linked this to the *water solenoid valve*. This means that the solenoid valve can be controlled to be opened automatically.

The TDS controller also has a sensor to test water for purity. This purity level can be manually set and we use 200ppm (parts per million), which is very safe for drinking.

Once this value is reached, power is supplied to a *second solenoid valve* (*TDS Valve*), it OPENs and water flows into the freshwater tank.

When > 200ppm is sensed, the TDS cuts the power and the *TDS valve* CLOSES, stopping water to the freshwater tank, which is then vented overboard.

Low Pressure Pump (LPP)
The LPP and its ON light are controlled from this electrical bus.

The Clutch
Power to activate the clutch is controlled from this electrical bus.

Basic Set-up

	Part Number	(Actual) Manufacturer	Inlet Size	Outlet Size	Max Press
Membranes SW 2540 (2)	Filmtec SW30-2540	Americanro	-	-	1000psi
Housings FRP (2)	PVF 2540 1000psi	Americanro	1/2" NPTF	1/2" NPTF	1000psi
Housings FRP		Freshwater outlet	-	1/2" NPTF	1000psi
Filter Housing (2x10") + SS bracket		Clarencewaterfilters	3/4" BSP	3/4" BSP	100psi
Filer - 5 micron		Clarencewaterfilters	-	-	-
Filer - 20 micron		Clarencewaterfilters	-	-	-
Pressure Gauge	AS254RB1500	rodpierce@houston.rr.com	-	-	1500psi
HP Cat Pump	Cat 00241 Pump	EDI Distributors	1/2" NPTF	3/8" NPTF	1200psi
Cat Clutch	Cat 34961 Clutch	EDI Distributors	-	-	-
Cat Regulator	Cat 7070 1000psi	EDI Distributors	1/2" NPTF	3/4" NPTF	1000psi
Cat nut set	Cat 34090	EDI Distributors	-	-	-
Flow Meter	Blue-White F55375L 0.4 - 4 lpm	Rose Industrial Marketing, Inc.	3/8" NPTM	3/8" NPTM	200psi
Flow Meter	Blue-White F55375L 0 2 - 20 lpm	garycrose@msn.com	1/2" NPTM	1/2" NPTM	200psi
Low Pressure Pump	Jabsco Cyclone Model: 50830-2012 12v	Peter Snell - RW Basham	3/4" BSP	3/4" BSP	100psi
Raw Water Strainer	Shurflo 0 3/4" SS strainer	Peter Snell - RW Basham	3/4" BSP	3/4" BSP	100psi
Pressure Relief Valve	SS-R4M8F8	Ebay - pipedotor1207	1/2" NPTM	1/2" NPTF	1500psi
Pressure Relief Valve - Spring	177-13k-R4-C Purple Spring 750-1500psi	Supplier BNE 07 3256 2327	-	-	950psi

Automatics

	Part Number	Manufacturer
Autoflush unit		qwwinc.com
TDS Meter	Hanna TDS Mini Controller BL-983319-0	Ebay cmcgehee01@comcast.net
Solenoid Valves		
		Subtotal

Other Filters and Componets

	Part Number	Manufacturer
Spare O-rind for housing (2)		Clarencewaterfilters
Filter Housing Spanner		Clarencewaterfilters
Undersink Filter Housing - Testa Twin		Clarencewaterfilters
U'sink Filters - GTS1-10 silver carbon 2		Clarencewaterfilters
U'sink Filter - 0.5 micron poly spun 2		Clarencewaterfilters
Undersink Housing Spanner		Clarencewaterfilters
Spare 5 micron 2		Clarencewaterfilters
Spare 20 micron 2		Clarencewaterfilters
Filter Housing (1x10") + SS bracket		Clarencewaterfilters
Vacuum Gauge	302DFW-254A	rodpierce@houston.rr.com

Chapter Six:
System Operation and Maintenance

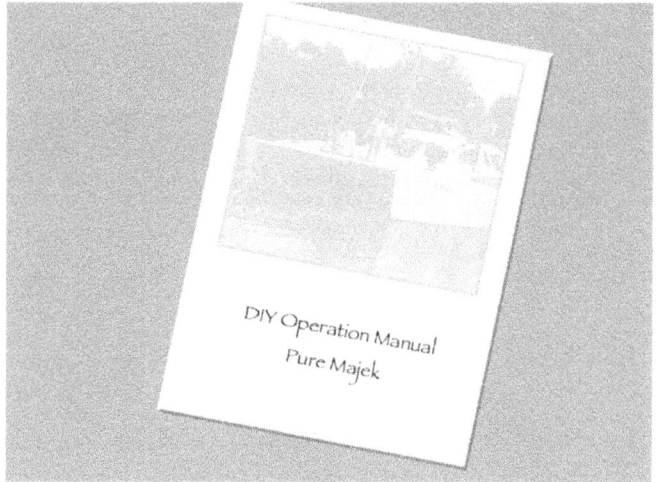

To prolong the life of all components, it is critical that clean water be used for the desalination process, even while testing the unit.

Chatting with Dow Corning (who make quality membranes), there preferred water quality is *'where you can see the bottom'*.

While a very broad comment, you can get the gist. Clean ocean flow is the preference, away from shore margins with mangroves.

----- : -----

It is assumed that the oil and fuel quantities have been checked and that all manufacturer data has been complied with in regard to the operation of their equipment.

Additionally that all filters are free of debris and that filters have been cleaned.

To Start:

1. OPEN the seawater inlet valve. Ensure that water is available at the LPP.

2. Ensure the Pressure Regulator is FULLY OPEN.

3. Ensure the Clutch is switched to OFF.

4. Turn ON the LPP and;
   > Confirm that low-pressure salt water is flowing through the system, watching the Brine Flow Meter

   (Note: This Flow Meter value needs to be ascertained early, noted and used at each start sequence).

5. START the Motor and;
   > Allow Motor to warm to

operating temperature, and

> Set 2500RPM, ensuring that the throttle is secured

(Note: It will slow back to 2400RPM with the clutch engaged. This value must not be exceeded for this engine).

6. ENGAGE the Clutch switch, and
a. SLOWLY CLOSE the Pressure Regulator. Monitor;
> The system pressure via the Pressure Gauge, 58 - 62bar (850 - 900psi) must be adhered too.

(Note: 62bar (900psi) MUST NOT be exceeded).

> Lock this setting with the 'Regulator Lock Nut'.

Continue to monitor this setting at regular intervals adjusting as required. (Note: a drop of more than 15% of a set value is an indication of soiled filters or a blockage. This can be confirmed against the Vacuum Gauge setting increasing).

7. Monitor the TDS Gauge, at;
> 200ppm, the valve should open allowing fresh water to the tank.

To Stop:
1. DISENGAGE the clutch,
2. OPEN the pressure Regulator,
3. Switch OFF the LPP.
4. Switch OFF the Motor.

------ : -----

Pickling

The period that the membranes should be left unattended (being no flow) varies from manufacturer to manufacturer.

They are all clear though on one issue, that is that the membranes are temperamental and need all the pampering they can get.

Left unattended for just four days with no flow allows the fluids to settle, stagnate and provide active fertile grounds for bacterial growth.

To counter this, two things can be done. Either cycle the system for one minute with either fresh or saltwater, or 'Pickle' the system.

Pickling is normally left to periods of extended duration because of the effort required to set-up and then cleans out, and we have chosen periods of more than two months, as our benchmark.

If we intend having the desalinator inactive for this long, we would consider pickling.

The 'Pickle' is basically a liquid preservative. The liquid solution is then fed through the system from beginning to end and left to do its job.

It should also be noted that to restart the unit and have available fresh unpreserved water, it should be left running for 1 hour, even if the TDS indicates good water quality.

The pickling solution can and does cause headaches, diarrhoea and in some cases joint swelling.

The most common preservative is Sodium Metabisulphite. Chemists, local brewery houses, and some chain supermarkets sell this powder as it's used in the beer or wine markets.

Mix 1/2 cup of Sodium Metabisulphite with 15 litres of

freshwater, and then put all the fluid except for the last 1/2 litre, through the system.

The fluid is pumped into the system via the pickling valve, with the freshwater valve closed and the'needle valve' turned to the full open position.

This ensures that all excess pickling fluid will vent overboard. As it nears the bottom of the pickle solution, stop and lock all systems.

Do not allow air to enter the piping system. This can then be left for extended periods.

----- : -----

Membrane storage

We have trialed a great way to store a membrane and have listed this on our diycatamaran.com website.

It really is a novel way of looking after a membrane other than running an automated system.

----- : -----

Chapter Seven:
ERS – Watermaker Rebuild

While conducting the monthly pilgrimage on Ebay, we spotted an auction for a well used Schenker Smart 30 desalinator.

Understanding that these quality Italian made watermakers retail from USD$4500 upwards, we tracked the progress of bidding with interest.

In the end we managed to win (sight unseen), the complete package for USD$700 (including postage). And its here that this document begins.

----- : -----

General

Schenker watermakers are manufactured in Italy with agents strategically positioned around the world.

They use an ERS assembly system (Energy Recovery System) which in short allows for 'low pressure water pumping' while utilising high-pressure membranes.

The internal dual-piston uses the intake low-pressure water (on one side of the piston) to build high-pressure water on the other side of the piston and presents this higher-pressure water to the membrane.

The spent (or brine water) from the membrane (still under pressure) is then returned and presented to the reciprocal ERS piston.

The two pistons work in unison delivering energy to further pressurise water membrane intake water.

The pressure increase is amazingly

from 70psi - 800psi using this system.

It is a very clever, effective, and smart way of using hydraulics to your advantage while halving your energy consumption.

From the outset, it needs to be said that Schenker and its distributors in Britain and Australia were very helpful, a credit to Schenker.

For the world cruiser, this is a real asset in the event of malfunctions in difficult places. This unit can be worked on effectively with their help via written/email correspondence.

> *...surprisingly got a prompt reply from a very helpful Ricardo Verde...*

This unit reminds me of two others on the market that use similar techniques - Katadyn and Spectra.

----- : -----

Many of the components and TDS units and automatics used here are the same as those discussed earlier in this book.

----- : ------

So what's all the fuss about?

Two keys things:
> The only high-pressure sections are the membrane and hoses connecting that membrane pressures around 800-900psi.

The remainder of the unit uses low pressure - around 60-80psi.

>The only pump needed is a 12vDC saltwater pump that draws a maximum of 9A to produce 25lts o water (we discuss this 25lt and not 30lt further in this document).

The watermaker package is made up of two key components, the 'Watermaker Group' and the 'Pump Group'.

Simple connections of saltwater inlet, brine overflow, and freshwater outlet are all that are needed.

Understanding that the unit we had purchased, no longer had a warranty attached (given its age), we chose to expand on the unit's installation and add a few creature comforts.

----- : -----

The Pump Group

The old pump group had to all be discarded, including the 12vDC pump and electrics, so it was back to the drawing board using the theory presented earlier in this document.

Our 'new' pump group purchases included:
> 12vDC high-pressure pump (up to 150psi),

> Overpressure relief valve (Swagelok),

> Water Filters - 1 x 60micron and 1 x 5micron, and

> Fittings - various high pressure PVC fittings

----- : -----

The Watermaker Group

The purchased unit was relatively well in one piece. However, there were a lot of rust and apparent areas of leakage.

Additionally, we found a crack on one of the upper blocks, which we later found, presented no problem.

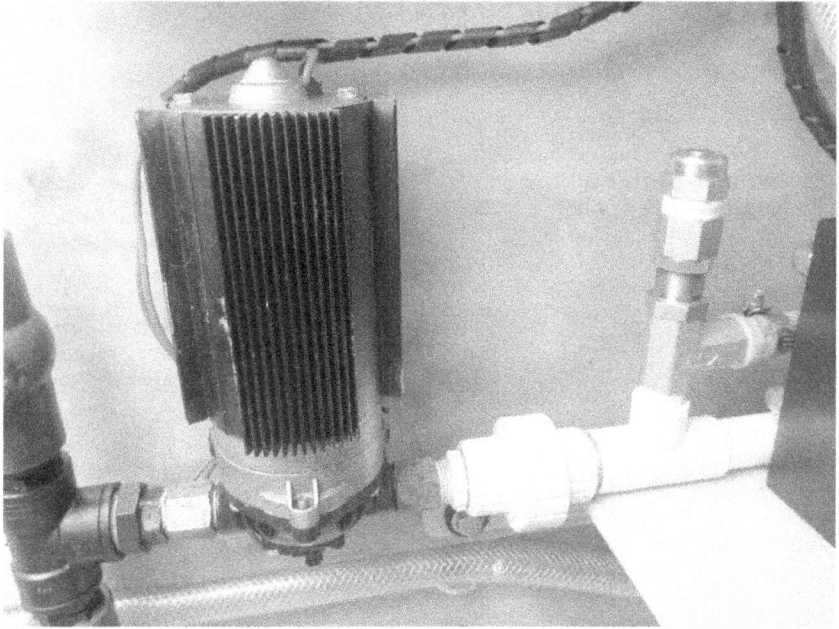

New 12vDC pump with cooling fans and Over Pressure Relief Valve

ERS Unit in place , membrane at the back and filters below.

Appears that the unit may have been dropped somewhere along its journey.

The work here included:
> Replacing all O-rings,
> Resealing all fitting points,
> Replacing a cylinder sleeve,
> Regreasing all internal areas (with exception to the 4 valves), and
> Replacing the membrane.

----- : -----

Disassembly and clean

Finding a 'Service Manual' on the Internet proved to be very difficult, even on the Schenker website. We sent an email directly to Schenker and surprisingly got a prompt reply from a very helpful Ricardo Verde.

This reply and attached documents proved to be our saviour.

The ERS unit has a million O-rings, many of which are not available from our normal sources, but are available through the agents of Schenker.

We can only encourage those rebuilding their units to have the Service Document at hand, especially with the valve components.

This is critical in re-assembly.

The greasing compound we chose to use was INOX MX6 with PTFE. It is a no melt, high temperature, extreme pressure, food grade premium machinery grease, highly resistant to water, salt, drying and chemicals.

----- : -----

Rebuild/Assembly

ERS Unit:

We found much of the corrosion to be surface corrosion. With the only exception being scarring inside one of the carbon-fibre sleeves (replacement part from Schenker).

We carefully wrote down the disassembly process, found that the ERS had been worked on previously, and not correctly put back together.

Of major concern was sand/grit found within the sleeve chamber around one of the pistons. This indicated a lack of saltwater filtration.

It also meant that damage might exist within other components.

We incorrectly greased these pieces when assembling and it wasn't until the 15th frustrating disassembly that we realised this problem.

We kept the old membrane for testing of leaks and water flow.

----- : -----

Membrane

We made contact with Dow and found a Filmtec membrane to suit.

The high-pressure membrane was ordered from Freshwater Systems (model SW 30-2521) in the USA.

Their delivery was also fast and efficient. Of interest was some information from Mactrashop (in Britain) about looking after the membranes and servicing from the opposition membrane maker Hydranautics.

ERS Unit - Sad Disrepair

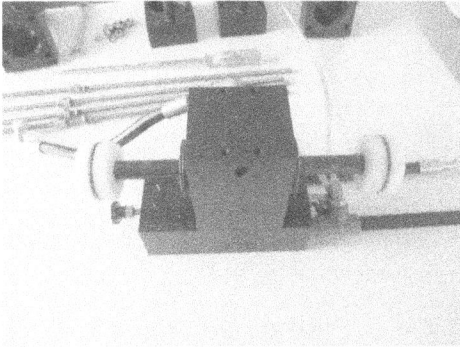

ERS Unit - Rebuilding from seals to stainless work

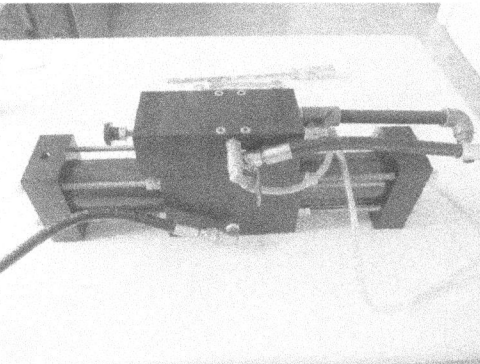

ERS Unit - Completing fore and aft connections

Together with that of Filmtec, we managed to get a good library for care and maintenance information.

----- : -----

Pump Group

We rebuilt the whole 'pump group' using our own components and consists of:
1. Filters (3),
2. Shurflo Pump
3. Shurflo Accumulator,
4. Control Box, and
5. Proportional Relief Valve.

...good thing about this motor is that it can run dry temporarily with no internal damage...

Filters:
The single Schenker filter was replaced with two new filters in very accessible positions away from the motor and electrical.

Plumbing was also large æî PVC high-pressure piping, removing the possibility of cracking and leaks, while allowing high volume water flow to the pump.

1 x 10-inch - 60-micron washable filter to remove larger solids. The key is the high flow rate of the filter.

The unit we have unscrews at the ends allowing the screen to be removed and washed.

This also negates the 'normal' filter at inlet point allowing direct water flow to the highest point of the Watermaker before adding hurdles like a filter.

1 x 10-inch - 5 micron poly-spun polypropylene filter mainly to remove sand, rust and algae. It is expected to replace these on a regular basis and the reason for a common brand and filter housing to contain the replacement cost.

The filter needs to have good debris holding capacity (which removes pleated filter types) and still allow high flow rates.

1 x 10î impregnated carbon filter to remove chlorine that may be in the tanks from town water top-ups.

While we have no concern with it in the tanks, it is the biggest no-no for the membranes of the desalinator in rinsing, in fact, it will 'kill' the membrane.

The Motor:
The only motor that suited our needs was the Shurflo 12vDC (Specifically - 8030-813-239), which we tracked down in the United States.

We eventually installed this unit upright to prevent any saltwater flow over the pump.

The installation inlet sits 1 meter from the seacock, almost at its upper lift point of 1.2 meters.

The other good thing about this motor is that it can run dry temporarily with no internal damage.

Rated at 9A, it is a high power consumer however; we later show this to be at its very upper limit.

Over-pressure relief Valve:
We found a Swagelok proportional relief valve (R series) on Ebay (got a mixed set of 6 for $20US used).

This is the same valve discussed in the 'Watermaker Component' parts area earlier in the volume.

Filters (5 and 10 micron)

Carbon Filter, Shurflo Pump
(bottom), Accumulator (right)

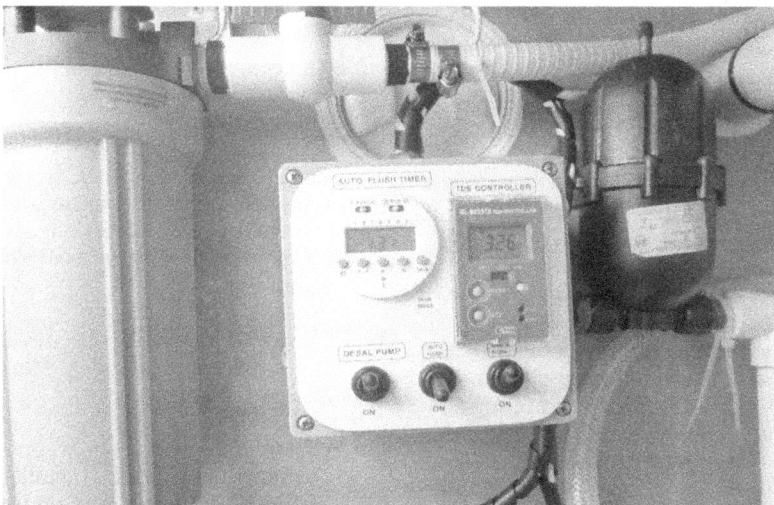

Auto-Flush Controller installed - 3-switches, TDS controller and
timer

The reason we went this way was for the quality brand and stainless steel build. While the pressure can be preset and lock-wired, we preferred the option of manual control.

This is available with this particular type by screwing the top and then locking with a nut.

This allowed us to easily vary the pressure release as the membrane and filters age.

----- : -----

The Electrical connection

Here we made some advanced changes by automating the flush system.

The control box has a timer, TDS meter, and three switches.

The timer is installed for controlling the æî 12vDC valve to allow freshwater from the vessels freshwater system to clean and flush the ERS and membrane automatically.

It utilised the vessels pressure system, so did not require the Shurflo pump to operate during this cycle.

It was also necessary to install a carbon filter to remove chlorine from the flush system (discussed in the 'filter section'), prior to entering the ERS units. This is a critical inclusion.

The TDS meter was from Hanna Instruments (BL 983319-0) and is also 12vDC operated with a connection to a æî valve that allows auto-switching from the overboard outlet to the freshwater tank inlet, when the desalinated water is suitable for drinking.

In our case we have set the value to 175ppm, but this can be higher (around 200ppm) without a salty taste.

One other thing to remember here is that the instrument does not come with the Hanna TDS Probe (HI 7634-00) and needs to be ordered separately.

The three switches control:
> Shurflo 12vDC pump (main switch to operate the desalinator),
> Flush Auto Timer (to switch the timer to 'auto' mode) with 2A CB, and
> Flush Manual Switch (to manually flush the unit).

This electrical box is then wired into our ships Hot Battery Bus (the electrical bus that is 'hot' when we leave the vessel) via a 9A CB.

----- : -----

Accumulator

An accumulator in essence is there to dampen pressure surges within the water system.

The ERS pistons switch from left to right around every 6 seconds and this change in direction causes momentary surges within the plumbing.

This is dampened with the Shurflo Accumulator (model 182) pre-charged to 40psi.

Given that water may enter the chamber, we have installed this higher than normal and with the air outlet toward the top for easy access.

In our photos, you may see a darkened discolouration on many of our components including the Shurflo pump.

This is deliberate as we are huge fans of Tectyl 506.

We use a lot of this on the yacht and cover anything that can come into contact with the elements (it dries brown and translucent in colour and lasts for many years).

Testing Home:

We tested the system at home using the old membrane and fresh tank water all screwed onto a basic frame. Using an Esky, we then introduced the saltwater - tuning the system to suit.

During the restart process, Jim from Mactrashop assisted us and pointed out that we needed to improve the fresh water with salt to provide more accurate pumping action pressure.

'With seawater you will get a greater pressure as it is denser than fresh water. If you mix fresh water with sea salt at 35g per litre, you can replicate this'.

This was key in balancing the operating pressure.

Even after this, we found the unit lacking consistent movement and again Mactrashop came to the rescue.

The accumulator was very low on pre-charge; this was pumped up using a bicycle pump to 40psi. It wasn't until these tweaks were accomplished that the unit performed, as it should.

Given that the unit appeared 'well used' and that components may have worn (due to neglect with the filters), we were expecting around 15lt/hour.

After running the ERS in for an hour,

we changed the membrane to a new membrane and the testing showed 18lt/hr.

----- : -----

On-board

The motor consistently draws 6.5A - 7.5A and delivers 15-20lts per hour.

The electric valves draw 0.2A and are the 'Normally Closed' type (i.e. they only draw power when they are activated to open and as a safety feature, will therefore close if power is lost.

The flush module delivers 14psi - 20psi consistently, well below the maximum of the pump operation limit of 30psi.

The flush cycle uses 7lt per 4-minute freshwater flush and we have this set on a Tuesday and Saturday flush cycle.

During operation, the unit produces 15 litres per hour, not bad for the old girl.

To date the support from Mactrashop and Schenker watermakers has been first class.

We expect to get use out of our watermaker but note that it does take some effort to keep everything in good order.

----- : -----